Contemplating

GOD

in Salvation

Contemplating GOD in Salvation

A Devotional

LAWRENCE KIMBROUGH

BROADMAN
&HOLMAN
PUBLISHERS

NASHVILLE, TENNESSEE

Ten-digit ISBN: 0-8054-4086-0
Thirteen-digit ISBN: 978-0-8054-4086-7

Published by Broadman & Holman Publishers
Nashville, Tennessee

Dewey Decimal Classification: 234
Subject Heading: GOD \ SALVATION \
DEVOTIONAL LITERATURE

1 2 3 4 5 6 7 8 9 10   10 09 08 07 06

CONTENTS

INTRODUCTION

I f we've ever limited salvation to a one-time event, to a one-dimensional word that means something special in church but not too much on the sidewalks and subway stations of real life, we've left a whole lot out of our understanding.

Salvation is big. Like God is big. Like our souls and our plans and our futures are big.

It's been the cry of God's people from the Egyptian soldier side of the Red Sea, from the darkest days of oppression and exile, from the hushed, prophetless years leading up to the night in Bethlehem that a star shone and shepherds quaked.

And it remains today—the one thing our human hearts crave more than any other, though disguised behind dress suits and Botox treatments, though ordered to leave rather than be dealt with and received.

Safety. Confidence. Purpose. Hope. Home. Salvation.

As Christians, these are all ours. In multiples of millions. Tasted now in sips and swallows but soon to be ours by crate and shipload. The intent of these devotional times is to let the salvation of God we currently hold by the handful rush over us mind, soul, and spirit—beyond questions, problems, and suffering—until we find our rest in his eternal embrace.

Not just then but this afternoon.

What to Expect

These devotional moments on the promises and aspects of God's salvation are yours to use in whatever fashion you desire. And although I'm sure you'll find your own way to make this book work best for you, I thought I'd give you just a few ideas.

Most days don't lend themselves to a lot of quiet time with God. But then again, there are *some* days—perhaps early Sunday mornings, or a quiet afternoon, or the night before your day off—when you could really invest some extra time into worship, prayer, and Bible reading.

I'm thinking this collection of expanded devotionals would be perfect for that, especially because they include a whole bunch of related Scriptures to look up. That'll give God's Word a lot of opportunity to soak in.

Or perhaps you're the leader of some kind of Bible study—perhaps a men's prayer group or a handful of families who get together at someone's house once a week or so. This book ought to be a nice fit for you, then, because it keeps you on theme for a fairly long period of time and doesn't leave you short on material after five minutes. It's not too much, not too little. Maybe it'd be just right for you.

But again, *you're* the one who knows best what you need. You're the one God has made eager to dive deeper into this gift he's bought and delivered to you, hungry to know more of who he is, what he's done, what he's doing.

And where we're going with all this righteousness inside.

ONE

TRUE LOVE

Boy meets girl in his second year of college, her first. Pretty soon he's going out of his way to be where she is—her dorm building, the lunchroom, the sidewalk she's usually on after her 2:00 English class.

They start dating, it gets serious, and within eighteen months they're engaged. And two weeks after his graduation, they're married in her hometown church with three hundred guests, five sets of attendants, and a passing summer shower that lets up just as they're pulling away, arcing into a double rainbow that frames their departure in dreamlike shades of destiny.

And everyone calls that "love."

Yes, there's a lot to be said and celebrated about a love that ignites in young adulthood and leads to a lifelong marriage of "better or worse" commitment. But it's one thing to fall for a beautiful brunette or a handsome upper classman at the campus pizza shop. It's quite another for God to see us in all our wretchedness, itching to avoid him at every opportunity, despising "the riches of His kindness" (ROM. 2:4) . . .

And to love us anyway.

Father, I'll never understand the depth of love that led you to sacrifice your Son for me. But may I receive it with never-ending amazement.

3

Blessed be the God and Father of our Lord Jesus Christ, who has blessed us with every spiritual blessing in the heavens, in Christ; *for He chose us in Him, before the foundation of the world,* to be holy and blameless in His sight. In love He predestined us to be adopted through Jesus Christ for Himself, according to His favor and will, to the praise of His glorious grace that He favored us with in the Beloved.

In Him we have redemption through His blood, the forgiveness of our trespasses, according to the riches of His grace that He *lavished on us with all wisdom and understanding.* He made known to us the mystery of His will, according to His good pleasure that He planned in Him for the administration of the days of fulfillment—to bring everything together in the Messiah, both things in heaven and things on earth in Him.

In Him we were also made His inheritance, predestined according to the purpose of the One who *works out everything in agreement with the decision of His will,* so that we who had already put our hope in the Messiah might bring praise to His glory.

Your salvation may have happened on a bright Sunday morning when you were eight years old. Or on a weekend retreat when the message of the gospel first pierced the self-centered skin of your teenaged soul. Or alone in your bedroom one night when your sins came crashing down around you like tiles falling from the ceiling.

But let me tell you something even better than that: the plan that set up your salvation was in the mind and heart of God before he even spoke one single trout or tree leaf into existence. Though your acceptance of Christ's redemption has been "revealed at the end of the times for you," God's love on your behalf was already in full force and action "before the foundation of the world" (1 Pet. 1:20).

Now here we are already, toying around with the theological concepts of God's foreknowledge and predestination. But don't let those words scare you, if they do. None of us really come anywhere close to understanding all that God has done for us in Christ or how salvation actually works in the human heart.

But we do know this much from the Scriptures: "You, LORD, are our Father; from ancient times, Your name is our Redeemer" (ISA. 63:16). What has happened in our hearts first came to light in his. It has been his love reaching down, not our hopes reaching up, that has made this eternal transaction possible.

> READ
> 1 PETER 1:18–21

OLD-TIME RELIGION

How sad that so many in the world today think of him only as the God of seemingly senseless judgment, portraying him as the spinner of cyclones rather than the Savior of sinners. If they only knew that God has been in the saving business throughout every century of human history.

Even in Eden, with his first man and woman scrambling for fig leaves, it was the Lord himself who came calling to them, initiating a covenant of salvation to deal with their sin and rebellion. It was God who drew up the plans for Noah's ark, extending his promise of rescue to a race he could have just as easily destroyed but chose instead to redeem.

Abraham. Isaac. Jacob. Joseph. None of these men were mountains of strength. They needed little help getting themselves into their own troubles and fixes. Yet God's grace was on full display even in their Old Testament hearts—sparing them, securing them, saving them.

And, of course, few if any events paint a more vivid picture of God's salvation than the Passover deliverance from Egypt, when chained for generations to a hopeless stake of slavery, Israel found itself in the liberating arms of a soul-seeking God, springing them free for the promised land.

Truly, "God my king is from ancient times, performing saving acts on the earth" (Ps. 74:12).

READ
PSALM 44:4–8

ENDLESS LOVE

Apparently, since God hasn't chosen to tell us more than we need to know, the most important thing about salvation is not how it happens but that it happens at all. The illogic of a perfectly intact, self-sufficient Trinity, choosing to create and to involve himself/ themselves in the messy details of our lives, should send us to our knees in gaping wonder and worship.

For some reason—defined only by our word *love*, but certainly vast enough to fill its own dictionary—God has added to our vocabulary the word *salvation*. He has provided it to us not because we were smart enough to know we needed it but because saving us is in his nature.

"Love consists in this: not that we loved God, but that He loved us and sent His Son to be the propitiation for our sins" (1 JOHN 4:10), the means by which God's wrath could be justifiably turned away from us to attack our sin instead.

This makes his salvation the ultimate validation of your value. The one who could have rightfully chosen to withhold life from you has not only created you but has recreated you, transforming you from an eighty-years-if-you're-lucky person into an eternal trophy of his grace.

And *that's* what true love is.

READ
ROMANS 5:6–11

DIG IN

The epic language of Ephesians 1 makes our salvation so much more certain and glorious than we often imagine it.

"HE CHOSE US IN HIM, BEFORE THE FOUNDATION OF THE WORLD" (V. 4). How does it feel to know that your life has a purpose as old as time itself and a God who won't let you forget it?

....

....

....

....

....

"IN HIM WE HAVE REDEMPTION . . . LAVISHED ON US WITH ALL WISDOM AND UNDERSTANDING" (VV. 7-8). What proves to you that salvation is no risky proposition but a thought-out plan?

....

....

....

....

....

"[HE] WORKS OUT EVERYTHING IN AGREEMENT WITH THE DECISION OF HIS WILL" (V. 11). Love is a choice, the experts say and our experience bears out. Why would God choose to love us?

....

....

....

....

....

Contemplating God in Salvation Over and Over Again

1. **Salvation has always been God's plan for us.**
   The love we have for our children—a love that begins long before we ever hold them in our arms—is about as close as we can come to understanding how God could love us in our sinful state. But because we are his and because he is love, we can rest in his eternal plan. Anyone who would think of us so far in advance is well worth our trust.

2. **Salvation is made possible only through Christ.**

3. **Salvation must be received in total dependence.**

4. **Salvation is the ultimate adoption procedure.**

5. **Salvation gives us access to the Holy Spirit.**

6. **Salvation results in the forgiveness of our sins.**

7. **Salvation saves us from more than we realize.**

8. **Salvation continues to grow and transform us.**

9. **Salvation should be a constant source of joy.**

10. **Salvation is best experienced in community.**

11. **Salvation crosses all borders and boundaries.**

12. **Salvation is meant to be shared with others.**

13. **Salvation is an everlasting covenant with God.**

14. **Salvation culminates in a future-tense event.**

Pray About

- Gaining a greater appreciation for the cost of your salvation.
- Learning how to feel secure in the all-wise hands of God.
- How to encourage others with God's love for them in Christ.

TWO

THE ONE, THE ONLY

Most of us are well beyond having a problem with the fact that Jesus Christ is "the way"—the *only* way—that "no one comes to the Father except through" the Son (JOHN 14:6). Don't ever stop being grateful for possessing that kind of faith.

Our more pressing problem, actually, is trying to express this truth in a world where one way is never enough. It's not *being* a Christian that troubles us; it's having to defend a doctrine that so many people find archaic, ludicrous, or downright conceited.

I mean, we're people who don't often take no for an answer. Show us an application deadline of two days ago, and we'll still call to see if tomorrow would be OK. At a recent orchestra concert my daughter was playing in, when they announced that any personal video recording would be "strictly prohibited," I stopped counting the tripods and handheld cameras at twelve.

No way does our culture like "one way."

So what's a Christian to do—one who believes this but is not so sure anyone else will?

Lord Jesus, you have convinced me through your Word and your Spirit that this is true. Help me not only to believe it but to live it.

These things having been set up this way, the priests enter the first room repeatedly, performing their ministry. But the high priest alone enters the second room, and that only once a year, and never without blood, which he offers for himself and for the sins of the people committed in ignorance. The Holy Spirit was making it clear that *the way into the holy of holies had not yet been disclosed* while the first tabernacle was still standing. . . .

Now the Messiah has appeared, high priest of the good things to come. In the greater and more perfect tabernacle not made with hands (that is, not of this creation), *He entered the holy of holies once for all,* not by the blood of goats and calves, but by His own blood, having obtained eternal redemption.

For if the blood of goats and bulls and the ashes of a heifer sprinkling those who are defiled, sanctify for the purification of the flesh, *how much more will the blood of the Messiah,* who through the eternal Spirit offered Himself without blemish to God, *cleanse our consciences from dead works* to serve the living God?

If anyone ever tells you they have a hard time believing the Bible because it's so full of errors and inconsistencies, my pal Bill Fay has the best response I've ever heard. "Using all the love you can muster," he says, "hand your friend a copy of the Bible and ask, 'Would you show me one?'"

Now obviously people can be at a point where they don't put any more stock in the Scripture's authority than they do the promises made in a presidential debate. But they could search high and low through every book, chapter, and page of the Bible, and they won't find any compromising on the fact that God has established one way of salvation.

Certainly, it would be a lot more comforting if we could believe that every Super Bowl athlete who's ever thanked God from the trophy platform knew who he was talking about. We could wish that every person who performed a selfless act of sacrifice or a daring deed of wartime bravery recognized where their guts and glory really came from.

But Christians are called upon to be culturally incorrect enough not to exclude or feel superior to anyone else but to hold to the one truth that's truly strong enough to hold us.

There are no alternatives. There are no other ways. To profess otherwise is to lie and call it love.

READ
ACTS 4:8–12

ALWAYS THE ONE

Interestingly enough, this "one way" reality comes through just as powerfully and prophetically in the Old Testament as it does in the New.

David, who had the raw skills and cunning to bring down a lion or a bear with his own two hands, learned from personal experience to "rest in God alone, my soul, for my hope comes from Him. He alone is my rock and my salvation, my stronghold; I will not be shaken" (Ps. 62:5–6).

Isaiah's spirit cried out in agreement with the words God had planted in his ears: "There is no other Savior but Me" (ISA. 43:11). And because there wasn't a man to be found who could sponsor and bring this deliverance to Israel—"no one interceding" on their helpless behalf—"so His own arm brought salvation, and His own righteousness supported Him" (ISA. 59:16).

The prophet Hosea, who had been taught through wildly extraordinary circumstances what it meant to love the most unlovely and wayward of all, could echo God's voice in saying, "You know no God but Me, and no Savior exists besides Me" (HOS. 13:4).

And though "falsehood comes from the hills"—as readily today as in the age of Jeremiah—"the salvation of Israel" and of all

God's people "is only in the LORD our God" (JER. 3:23).

READ ZECHARIAH 9:9–10

Then. Now. Forevermore.

A TIME TO BELIEVE

But we need to be patient with those who are having a hard time dealing with this crosscurrent of natural opinion.

Jesus was.

We get to watch this happening to a well-connected Pharisee named Nicodemus, who, of course, came to Jesus at night, trying to deal with the confusion he felt toward this Man who seemed to be challenging every religious thought he'd ever accepted. Yet he felt strangely drawn to him, wanting to believe, at least when we wasn't wanting not to.

You know well the transcript of their encounter, the "born again" idea that fell so heavily on Nicodemus's ears, the John 3:16 promise of eternal life to those who believe in the One, the Son, the only begotten of the Father.

Their after-hours discussion didn't end in a dramatic conversion or a rush to the river for baptism. Jesus didn't press him into a confession or threaten to blackball him for not immediately believing.

Instead, we see Nicodemus later, in John 7:50–51, mildly standing up for Christ, enduring the sarcastic slander of his own kind for giving Jesus the benefit of the doubt. By the time of John 19:39, however, Nicodemus had apparently come full circle, toting "75 pounds of myrrh and aloes" to pay homage to the dead body of Christ.

Truly, salvation through Jesus alone can only be accepted as the

READ JOHN 3:13–21

Holy Spirit opens people's hearts to receive him. Our job is not to convince, just to convey.

DIG IN

We may be unfamiliar with the priestly offices described in Hebrews 9. But we know we need more than "dead works."

"THE WAY INTO THE HOLY OF HOLIES HAD NOT YET BEEN DISCLOSED" (v. 8). What do you think God's purposes were in establishing and carrying out the regulations of the old covenant?

....
....
....
....
....

"HE ENTERED THE HOLY OF HOLIES ONCE FOR ALL" (v. 12). What was different about Christ's blood? What made it more effective than "the blood of goats and calves"?

....
....
....
....
....

"HOW MUCH MORE WILL THE BLOOD OF THE MESSIAH . . . CLEANSE OUR CONSCIENCES FROM DEAD WORKS . . . ?" (v. 14). How have "dead works" taken their toll on your life and your spirit?

....
....
....
....
....

Contemplating God in Salvation Over and Over Again

1. SALVATION HAS ALWAYS BEEN GOD'S PLAN FOR US.

2. SALVATION IS MADE POSSIBLE ONLY THROUGH CHRIST.
Jesus alone is "the source of eternal salvation" (HEB. 5:9). You can play around with other theories or suppositions of your own for a while, but ultimately—according to the clear message of the Scriptures—it is only "Christ in you" that assures you "the hope of glory" (COL. 1:27). God has made a way to eternal rest, and that way is through his Son.

3. SALVATION MUST BE RECEIVED IN TOTAL DEPENDENCE.

4. SALVATION IS THE ULTIMATE ADOPTION PROCEDURE.

5. SALVATION GIVES US ACCESS TO THE HOLY SPIRIT.

6. SALVATION RESULTS IN THE FORGIVENESS OF OUR SINS.

7. SALVATION SAVES US FROM MORE THAN WE REALIZE.

8. SALVATION CONTINUES TO GROW AND TRANSFORM US.

9. SALVATION SHOULD BE A CONSTANT SOURCE OF JOY.

10. SALVATION IS BEST EXPERIENCED IN COMMUNITY.

11. SALVATION CROSSES ALL BORDERS AND BOUNDARIES.

12. SALVATION IS MEANT TO BE SHARED WITH OTHERS.

13. SALVATION IS AN EVERLASTING COVENANT WITH GOD.

14. SALVATION CULMINATES IN A FUTURE-TENSE EVENT.

PRAY ABOUT

- Any doubts you may have about the truth of the Scriptures.
- Your heart for those who are unwilling to believe in him.
- Your response to Christ for opening the door of salvation.

THREE
BAD TO THE BONE

Some of the doctrines of salvation (at least in their more in-depth, super-duper forms and expressions) can be a little hard to understand. Not everyone agrees with everything, and some points are harder to prove than others.

But when it comes to the notion of our own depravity, our inborn wickedness and need for Christ's salvation in the first place, our lives are Exhibit A every single day.

Pick a subject. Watch the news. Rent a movie. Visit the shopping mall. Everywhere around us, for as far as the eye can see, life daily digs up heaping handfuls of source material that verify what the Bible's been saying all along. In ways that are both sinister and subtle, bald-faced and backdoor, sin and all its nasty side effects populate just about every square inch of ground on God's green Earth.

Even we who've been redeemed, who through absolutely no good looks or leverage of our own have been counted totally righteous in God's eyes—even we continue systematically to fail and break his heart.

Our total dependence on him is simply an undeniable fact of life.

Lord God, help me never to become so accustomed to salvation that I forget how desperately I need it . . . even now.

Indeed, the LORD's hand is not too short to save, and His ear is not too deaf to hear. But *your iniquities have built barriers between you and your God,* and your sins have made Him hide His face from you so that He does not listen. For your hands are defiled with blood, and your fingers with iniquity; your lips have spoken lies, and you mutter injustice. No one makes claims justly; no one pleads honestly. *They trust in empty and worthless words;* they conceive trouble and give birth to iniquity. They hatch viper's eggs and weave spider's webs. Whoever eats their eggs will die; crack one open, and a viper is hatched. Their webs cannot become clothing, and *they cannot cover themselves with their works.* Their works are sinful works, and violent acts are in their hands. Their feet run after evil, and they rush to shed innocent blood. Their thoughts are sinful thoughts; ruin and wretchedness are in their paths. They have not known the path of peace, and there is no justice in their ways. They have made their roads crooked; no one who walks on them will know peace.

Ahh, little babies. Their working eyelashes and tiny fingernails. Their cherubic faces and chubby leg rolls. The powdery smell at the top of their heads. Perhaps nothing else in life is just the right size, just the right weight, just the right feel of a newborn baby.

But for all of that purity and preciousness, you have to believe—from what happens so soon thereafter—that as Augustine said, "The so-called innocence of children is more a matter of weakness of limb than purity of heart."

If they could pull the house down, they probably would.

And so begins a parent's start-up lesson in what God has had to deal with every single day since Adam and Eve chose badness over blessing. Even given the ideal environment, the primary colors in the nursery, the proper amount of sunlight, children will become problem-causers without even trying hard.

And, yes, we love our children. They bring us such joy and delight. Each of them is different. Each of them touches us in such fulfilling, heartwarming ways. But still, they are little sinners who grow into bigger sinners until God steps in and declares them saved sinners.

Not one of us receives salvation until we realize that without the grace of God, we'll never be anything more than a dressed-up deception machine.

READ
PSALM 36:1–9

FROM THE GROUND UP

This is why the only way to receive him is to realize our need for him. "For whoever keeps the entire law, yet fails in one point, is guilty of breaking it all" (JAMES 2:10). So "all who rely on the works of the law are under a curse" (GAL. 3:10)—the curse of forever falling short, standing naked before a holy God, being forced to admit to our eternal shame the condemning guilt of our hands and hearts.

Some stripes of Christendom are accused (perhaps rightly so) of bearing down too hard on this distasteful truth. The "cold, bad sinner" routine doesn't exactly put you in the mood for Sunday brunch, not the way a good "up with people" sermon can do.

But as Martin Luther wrote, "God creates out of nothing. Therefore until a man is nothing, God can make nothing out of him."

The essence of salvation is surrender. All the things we lean on to make our way in the world—our family connections, our good name, our handsome wardrobe, our skill at talking our way into people's affections—none of this matters. Until "Christ is all and in all" (COL. 3:11), we're not ready to be his disciples.

"You will be delivered," Isaiah wrote, only "by returning and resting; your strength will lie in quiet confidence" (30:15)—

the confidence of knowing that only God can make anything worthwhile out of our lives.

Until we're there, we still have a ways to go.

READ
JAMES 4:7–10

STILL TO COME

And even after conversion we remain totally dependent on our dependence. Whenever our pride thumbs its own suspenders, whenever we feel entitled to a few scraggly sins, whenever our self-reliance drapes itself in the American dream, we choke out the life of Christ in us. We choose to live with restricted airways. We find ourselves fatigued and just figure it's normal.

It's not.

Normal Christian living means daily receiving Christ's righteousness, regularly repenting of sin, continually relying on the grace of God—just as we did the hour we first believed.

Trying to pin the badge of faith onto raw flesh will never stop resulting in needless pain, sleepless nights, and spiritual frustration. The humility that first brought us to Christ will be the humility that keeps us close, keeps us tender, keeps us clothed in his purity and able to wear his name on our left pocket lapel.

I know that those who try encouraging us to believe in ourselves have every intention of inspiring us. Those who teach our children to dream big and remove their limitations are truly attempting to free them. But unless our belief is in Christ and our dreams are his, we will always be bypassing his promises and settling for pocket change.

READ
2 CORINTHIANS 7:8–11

DIG IN

The grim reminders of Isaiah 59 would be enough to depress us if God hadn't come up with a serious solution.

"YOUR INIQUITIES HAVE BUILT BARRIERS BETWEEN YOU AND YOUR GOD" (V. 2). How have these "barriers" been played out in your life? What have they cost? How have they hurt you?

....
....
....
....
....

"THEY TRUST IN EMPTY AND WORTHLESS WORDS" (V. 4). What are some of the "empty and worthless words" you hear today that come off sounding good but lie through their teeth?

....
....
....
....
....

"THEY CANNOT COVER THEMSELVES WITH THEIR WORKS" (V. 6). No, the "good works" thing doesn't work. But how do personal responsibility and dependence on Christ go together?

....
....
....
....
....

Contemplating God in Salvation Over and Over Again

1. Salvation has always been God's plan for us.

2. Salvation is made possible only through Christ.

3. Salvation must be received in total dependence. It's a good thing the Lord told us this, because we'd have never figured it out on our own: "All have sinned and fall short of the glory of God" (Rom. 3:23). This is the only kind of ground that salvation can grow in, the only kind of admission that can punch our ticket to paradise, the only kind of heart that gets to experience eternity . . . even while we're here.

4. Salvation is the ultimate adoption procedure.

5. Salvation gives us access to the Holy Spirit.

6. Salvation results in the forgiveness of our sins.

7. Salvation saves us from more than we realize.

8. Salvation continues to grow and transform us.

9. Salvation should be a constant source of joy.

10. Salvation is best experienced in community.

11. Salvation crosses all borders and boundaries.

12. Salvation is meant to be shared with others.

13. Salvation is an everlasting covenant with God.

14. Salvation culminates in a future-tense event.

Pray About

- How to express this truth to those who need to hear it.
- What dependence on Christ should look like in your life.
- The pockets of pride that need to be turned inside out.

FOUR

PUTTING
ON HEIRS

One of the most encouraging trends in recent history is the emergence of adoption as a widespread, well-accepted practice. Many children today—either abandoned or unwanted or born into abject poverty—are enjoying the grace of being loved, protected, and treasured in families.

May this continue to the glory of God.

But for those of us who've never adopted a child and aren't adopted ourselves, it's really hard to imagine how it feels to discover that your dad is not your birth father. Yes, he's the one who buys you ice cream, makes Saturday pancakes, and feeds the dog when you forget. But he's not really your blood relation, not the way some dads are.

Perhaps, though, an adopted child is able to come closer to embracing and being obedient to these unusual words of Jesus than some of the rest of us are: "Do not call anyone on earth your father, because you have one Father, who is in heaven" (MATT. 23:9)—the one who's adopted us in Christ and given us a richer, greater inheritance than any natural father could hope to bestow.

Yes, adoption is good, and by it we are all very blessed.

Father God, I could never earn your loving look and affection.
But I do recognize the grace in it and desire to be more thankful.

Those whose lives are in the flesh are unable to please God. You, however, are not in the flesh, but in the Spirit, since the Spirit of God lives in you. But *if anyone does not have the Spirit of Christ, he does not belong to Him.* Now if Christ is in you, the body is dead because of sin, but the Spirit is life because of righteousness. And if the Spirit of Him who raised Jesus from the dead lives in you, then He who raised Christ from the dead will also bring your mortal bodies to life through His Spirit who lives in you.

So then, brothers, *we are not obligated to the flesh to live according to the flesh,* for if you live according to the flesh, you are going to die. But if by the Spirit you put to death the deeds of the body, you will live. All those led by God's Spirit are God's sons. For you did not receive a spirit of slavery to fall back into fear, but *you received the Spirit of adoption, by whom we cry out, "Abba, Father!"* The Spirit Himself testifies together with our spirit that we are God's children, and if children, also heirs—heirs of God and co-heirs with Christ.

To attest that having children is hard, expensive, inconvenient, and routinely disruptive doesn't mean we're discouraging anyone from being a parent. Yet for all of its blessings and bear hugs and belly laughs, we'd be lying not to mention that parenthood also comes with teething tantrums, school clothes shopping, and a fair share of irrational conversations. Oh yeah, and lots of laundry.

What I'm saying is, God didn't have to put up with this parenting thing if he didn't want to.

And yet in ways that make pale by comparison any trouble our children can cause us, we have been (and continue to be) difficult kids for our Father to raise. We gripe. We complain. We make loud, vocal notice of his occasional silences, yet we regularly forget what he did for us just last week. We can be pretty incorrigible much of the time.

Yet for some reason God was not content with just being our Savior, merely sparing us from eternal doom (as if "merely" actually belongs in the same dependent clause with such incredible grace and mercy). He has chosen as well to become our *Father*, which makes us children born "not of blood, or the will of the flesh, or the will of man, but of God" (JOHN 1:13).

Yes, as part of being plucked out of Satan's grasp, we have also been received into God's precious family—not just hired into the organization, not just assigned an insider's pass code, not just placed on a master list somewhere.

> READ
> 1 JOHN 3:1–3

Loved. Accepted. Adopted.

UPROOTED FOR GOOD

Yet I wonder, even though we often refer to God as Father in our daily prayers and mealtime blessings, if we really think much about what that means.

In salvation we are actually lifted from our family of origin and placed into the family of God. That's why Jesus could make such radical statements as, "If anyone comes to Me and does not hate his own father and mother, wife and children, brothers and sisters—yes, even his own life—he cannot be My disciple" (LUKE 14:26).

In fact, when his own mom and siblings showed up one day looking for him, Jesus rather coldly rebuffed their intrusion, discounting their claim on his time. Turning to those who were seated with him, he said, "Who are My mother and My brothers? . . . Whoever does the will of God is My brother and sister and mother" (MARK 3:33, 35).

That's not to say, of course, that our blood relations suddenly become unimportant to us after salvation. Christ rebuked the Pharisees who piously withheld aid from their aging parents, men

23

who were more obsessed with giving to charity (and getting the credit) than caring for their own families (MARK 7:11–13).

Yet something revolutionary has happened in our spiritual DNA as a result of being saved from sin. Whatever our father has been like—whether good, bad, or disapprovingly indifferent—we now have a Father who is all-perfect, all-wise, all-loving, and altogether ours.

READ
LUKE 11:11–13

INHERITING A FORTUNE

But even more wonderful than having the Father of all fathers to call our own is the fact that he has written us into his will, ascribing the measure of his great wealth to our account.

Honestly, now, he really didn't have to do that!

Riches. Glory. The indwelling power of his precious Holy Spirit. The promise not only of eternal redemption but of heavenly reward for all the "gold, silver, costly stones" we allow him to produce in our lives (1 COR. 3:12).

There is no other explanation for this but divine love, the good pleasure of his own desire. It's not indulgence. It's not an open wallet and the car keys. He's not the easy touch that all those spoiled kids we grew up with had for parents.

But his generosity is lavish and extreme. It's enough to let us know full well, through what we've already received and what is even now laid away in store for us later, that we are children loved by a glorious God.

Or, as we're fond of calling him, Dad.

READ
GALATIANS 4:1–7

DIG IN

The life change and adoption procedure that occurred in our spirits at salvation is beautifully explained in Romans 8.

"IF ANYONE DOES NOT HAVE THE SPIRIT OF CHRIST, HE DOES NOT BELONG TO HIM" (V. 9). How do you experience the Spirit's presence in your life? What would it be like not to have him?

....
....
....
....
....

"WE ARE NOT OBLIGATED TO THE FLESH TO LIVE ACCORDING TO THE FLESH" (V. 12). Why do we often tend to feel "obligated" to follow up on temptation—almost entitled to a little sin?

....
....
....
....
....

"YOU RECEIVED THE SPIRIT OF ADOPTION, BY WHOM WE CRY OUT, 'ABBA, FATHER!'" (V. 15). This tender expression of family love seems almost irreverent. Is it? Why or why not?

....
....
....
....
....

Contemplating God in Salvation Over and Over Again

1. Salvation has always been God's plan for us.

2. Salvation is made possible only through Christ.

3. Salvation must be received in total dependence.

4. Salvation is the ultimate adoption procedure. "Blessed be the God and Father of our Lord Jesus Christ. According to His great mercy, He has given us a new birth into a living hope through the resurrection of Jesus Christ from the dead, and into an inheritance that is imperishable, uncorrupted, and unfading, kept in heaven for you" (1 Pet. 1:3–4). That ought to make you feel very loved right now.

5. Salvation gives us access to the Holy Spirit.

6. Salvation results in the forgiveness of our sins.

7. Salvation saves us from more than we realize.

8. Salvation continues to grow and transform us.

9. Salvation should be a constant source of joy.

10. Salvation is best experienced in community.

11. Salvation crosses all borders and boundaries.

12. Salvation is meant to be shared with others.

13. Salvation is an everlasting covenant with God.

14. Salvation culminates in a future-tense event.

Pray About

- Receiving God the Father's love and acceptance of you.
- Becoming more loving and accepting of other believers.
- Seeking to be increasingly grateful for God's grace.

FIVE
I CAN JUST FEEL IT

There are certain stripes of Christian thought that basically frown on feelings, people who primarily view their walk of faith in terms of endurance rather than enjoyment.

And we understand what they're guarding against. Heaven knows there are plenty of believers today who have more reverence for the New York Yankees than they do the King of glory.

But how cold and clinical it would have been for God to have wanted only to engage our minds, only to have given us books to read, only to have made us sit there and listen rather than to engage and interact, to enjoy his company.

And so he gave us his Spirit because he knows we are people who crave friendship, and fellowship, the feeling of sitting up late wanting to talk. He knows that clenched teeth and cloudy perceptions can only take us so far.

Truly, the deep feelings of joy and satisfaction we experience from salvation are the direct result of God's Holy Spirit in our lives. So let's be sure to remember where he lives and smile every time we think of it.

Holy Spirit, thank you for coming to live within me. May I seek to relish your presence and find real joy in your nearness.

In [Christ] *you also,* when you heard the word of truth, the gospel of your salvation—in Him when you believed—*were sealed with the promised Holy Spirit.* He is the down payment of our inheritance, for the redemption of the possession, to the praise of His glory.

This is why, since I heard about your faith in the Lord Jesus and your love for all the saints, I never stop giving thanks for you as I remember you in my prayers. I pray that the God of our Lord Jesus Christ, the glorious Father, *would give you a spirit of wisdom and revelation* in the knowledge of Him. I pray that the eyes of your heart may be enlightened so you may know what is the hope of His calling, what are the glorious riches of His inheritance among the saints, and *what is the immeasurable greatness of His power to us who believe,* according to the working of His vast strength.

He demonstrated this power in the Messiah by raising Him from the dead and seating Him at His right hand in the heavens—far above every ruler and authority, power and dominion, and every title given, not only in this age but also in the one to come.

One of the most touching insights into the heart of Jesus occurs in his John 17 prayer, a chapter that speaks so vividly of what Christlikeness is all about. Here he was, inches and hours from enduring the most cruelly unjust death in human history. And yet, in a prayer that runs for twenty-six red-letter verses in our modern Bibles, only five of those verses comprise his prayer for himself.

Even on the eve of his greatest suffering, his heart was on his friends.

You get the feeling as you read it that he'd have given almost anything if he could've stayed with them—not to escape, not so much because he feared the cross, but because he could see it in their eyes. He could sense what the strain was doing to them. He knew this was not the way they had ever thought this would end. The about-face appearance of Judas. The company of soldiers. The temple police. The lanterns, the swords, the torches.

For a brief moment—I hope this is not a stretch—Jesus must have felt more confined by his humanity than at any previous time in his earthly life. If only this once he could have allowed himself to be two places at one time: saving his people while also comforting his friends.

And that's why, in several places over the course of his long exchange with them in JOHN 14–16, he told them about the Holy Spirit—this one who would be revealed to them at a certain time, at the request of the Son, at the good pleasure of the Father.

> READ
> JOHN 14:15–18

I'LL BE THERE

"I will not leave you as orphans," Jesus said. "I am coming to you" (JOHN 14:18). Perhaps over the forty days after Christ's resurrection, those of his friends who remembered these precrucifixion words of Jesus thought perhaps they were already living the quick fulfillment of his promise. Yes, he had to die, but now he had risen up to walk with them afresh, like always.

How his ascension must have thrown them into confusion all over again.

Yet he did come. Again. In fire and power and a 9:00 a.m. infusion of new wine (ACTS 2:15). He would not leave them to struggle alone through the treacherous first days of a new, revolutionary age. He would be there. With them. Always.

And even today, when we receive him as Savior, we also receive him as Spirit. This "Counselor"—this "Spirit of truth"—this one who will "take from what is Mine and declare it to you" (JOHN 16:14) is the glorious, bedrock promise that encouraged the heart of Christ, even while clutched in the tight grip of Gethsemane.

He could pray for our futures and be assured of our provision because he knew that even when we couldn't see him, he'd be there.

READ
JOHN 16:7–13

We could feel him.

THE GIFT OF GOD

And each day, as we get to know his Spirit better, as we learn to recognize his voice, as we allow his will to override our own sense of now-or-never action and urgency, we feel him directing us, leading us, encouraging us.

When we're tempted to base all our decisions on how they affect a two-week time frame, he is the gift of far-reaching wisdom, of knowledge and insight that can see way beyond our own short-term hopes and desires. He may not make things perfectly clear to us—not the way we'd like him to—but we know he sees them clearly. And by submitting to him and trusting in his sovereign direction, we can remain at peace, confident that we're walking in his footsteps.

When we're tempted to minimize our talents and squander them on ourselves, he is the gift of new opportunity. He's the one who reveals to us the fruitlessness of watching reruns while life ticks by and eternity attempts to invade our living space. He's the one—if we'll let him—who shows us why writing a letter is a better use of our mind than complaining about how busy we are, why making a hospital visit occasionally needs to outrank our lunch plans, why sending a twenty-five-dollar check to a struggling friend fills a much deeper need in us than a new pair of slacks or a Kenny Chesney CD.

READ
2 CORINTHIANS
5:1–10

The Holy Spirit is God's gift to his people.

DIG IN

The high-sounding language of Ephesians 1 can actually be our everyday experience as we walk with the Spirit.

"IN HIM YOU ALSO . . . WERE SEALED WITH THE PROMISED HOLY SPIRIT" (V. 13). Why do some people, perhaps even you, often feel as though their salvation is dangling by a thread?

....
....
....
....
....

"WOULD GIVE YOU A SPIRIT OF WISDOM AND REVELATION IN THE KNOWLEDGE OF HIM" (V. 17). How is the dynamic of receiving his wisdom different from the normal five senses?

....
....
....
....
....

"WHAT IS THE IMMEASURABLE GREATNESS OF HIS POWER TO US WHO BELIEVE" (V. 19). What keeps us from feeling "immeasurable" and powerful? What would be different if we did?

....
....
....
....
....

Contemplating God in Salvation Over and Over Again

1. Salvation has always been God's plan for us.
2. Salvation is made possible only through Christ.
3. Salvation must be received in total dependence.
4. Salvation is the ultimate adoption procedure.
5. Salvation gives us access to the Holy Spirit.

   Oh, sure, part of the Spirit's job in us is to discipline and rebuke. We need that, he knows it, and he loves enough to consider our character more valuable than our comfort. But as our surrender to him grows more and more complete, our relationship with the Spirit of God will increasingly be one of joy, peace, and all those other good Galatians 5 things.

6. Salvation results in the forgiveness of our sins.
7. Salvation saves us from more than we realize.
8. Salvation continues to grow and transform us.
9. Salvation should be a constant source of joy.
10. Salvation is best experienced in community.
11. Salvation crosses all borders and boundaries.
12. Salvation is meant to be shared with others.
13. Salvation is an everlasting covenant with God.
14. Salvation culminates in a future-tense event.

Pray About

- What needs to quiet in you so you can hear his Holy Spirit.
- How to begin living in the freedom of what he's promised.
- The courage to follow up on the opportunities he reveals.

SIX
CLEAN THROUGH

There's always a chance that the forgiveness of our sins can become just another piece of furniture in our lives, one we can go weeks without noticing. Or nothing more than a tag-on phrase thrown in just before the end of our prayers, spoken with about as much sincerity as the "have-a-nice-day" you get at the drive-thru around 9:30 on a Friday night.

But I think one of the main reasons why this salvation essential becomes sadly old hat in our minds is because for a lot of us, it's been a long time since we've seen it break out on someone.

Get around a twenty-year-old junior in college who's been struggling with just about every sin you can think of but who's been drawn to a campus ministry through a classmate two doors down in the dorm. Look into the eyes of newfound forgiveness, and you'll remember what a prize God's mercy is.

So if ever forgiveness stops surprising you, it may be because you haven't talked with anyone about it in a while. It may be because the Spirit needs to place you in someone's life who needs it the way you once did, the way all of us do.

Dear Lord, if I haven't been moved to much worship lately by the righteousness you've given me, change my heart, wash me clean.

My soul, praise the LORD, and all that is within me, praise His holy name. My soul, praise the LORD, and do not forget His benefits.

He forgives all your sin; He heals all your diseases. He redeems your life from the Pit; He crowns you with faithful love and compassion. He satisfies you with goodness; your youth is renewed like the eagle.

The LORD executes acts of righteousness and justice for all the oppressed. He revealed His ways to Moses, His deeds to the children of Israel. The LORD is compassionate and gracious, slow to anger and full of faithful love. He will not always accuse us or be angry forever. *He has not dealt with us as our sins deserve or repaid us according to our offenses.*

For as high as the heavens are above the earth, so great is His faithful love toward those who fear Him. As far as the east is from the west, so far has He removed our transgressions from us. As a father has compassion on his children, so *the LORD has compassion on those who fear Him.* For He knows what we are made of, remembering that we are dust.

People respond to the forgiveness of God in different ways. Paul addressed a common reaction in Romans 6, when he mentioned those who drink Christ's mercy is like a free pass at Disneyland, a permission slip that entitles them to just about any attraction or concession stand they like.

There are other people, though, who can never quite accept the fact that his pardon is for them. They've done too much, they've been betrayed too often, they've continued to fail despite every seeming attempt at obedience. So while they can embrace the concept in theory, they rarely *feel* forgiven. It's hard for them to imagine that God could be that understanding.

Of course, there are some who just don't give the matter a whole lot of thought. Salvation and church attendance and the usual routine jumble into one big package that's been their way of life for so long, it's sort of been absorbed into the house paint. It's just the way things work.

But whether abused or disbelieved, overlooked or daily remembered, God's forgiveness of us in Christ is much bigger than our own perceptions of it. None of us fully understand the high price that was outlaid for us on the cross, nor the deep deliverance that was deposited into our account as a result.

Yet it was. And he did. And when we wake up every morning, we should never have too many conscious thoughts before *that* one pops into our head.

READ
ACTS 13:38–41

THE FACTS OF FORGIVENESS

Like most everything in our basic theology pack, forgiveness should never be confined to how it feels but rather accepted for what it is.

According to the Scriptures, God's mercy that covers us at conversion is like "pure water" poured over our heads and down to our feet. It has the power to cleanse us, not just from sinful acts, but from the debilitating drain of an "evil conscience" (HEB. 10:22). It is a total rinsing and refreshing, like a cannonball into the deep end, giving us immediate relief from every scorching sunbeam of an August afternoon.

It's also a fresh-paint experience, a "white as snow" shellacking over every square inch of dark walls and splotchy paneling (ISA. 1:18). My family once moved into a house whose bathrooms were lined in wallpaper that looked like a Kleenex box, the silver and gold foil tingeing everything in early seventies. Never have interior walls glowed more brightly than after tasting those top coats of white primer. The old was gone. And nothing was ever bringing it back.

Forgiveness, too, is an absolute gift, with no points added for good behavior or for a laudable time in the half marathon. It's not an earned income credit but a commodity given only "through faith in Christ" (PHIL. 3:9). This sounds so basic and simple, yet we do so easily forget that without him, nothing good shows up on our side of the ledger lines. Nothing. Every last payment for our forgiveness has come from an outside source. All we do is just sit back and enjoy.

READ
ROMANS 3:24–26

FREEDOM RING

The big Bible word for this (you probably know) is *justification*, the belief that God has squared his books and considered us forgiven. He has passed sentence on our sin by accepting Christ's sacrifice and is therefore totally within his own consistent standards to declare us righteous in his sight.

And so we are.

And so we can act like it. We can hear the guilty accusations of our own past thoughts and memories and dismiss them as irrelevant. We can feel the tug of temptation on our spirits but submit our struggle into Christ's capable hands and watch victory beget victory. We can throw our full weight on God's compassion and lose our fear of being found out or exposed, for "who can bring an accusation against God's elect? God is the One who justifies" (ROM. 8:33).

Being forgiven (and knowing it) means that freedom—real freedom—could be on your doorstep in the morning. It could stare back at you from the bathroom mirror. It could put a deep breath of relief back into your marriage, your family life, all your relationships. It could turn you loose to serve God as never before.

That's the power of being clean.

READ
PSALM 51:7–13

DIG IN

If you ever catch yourself with your Bible open but not sure which chapter to read, Psalm 103 is always a good place to go.

"He forgives all your sin; He heals all your diseases" (v. 3). In what way is sin like a disease in our lives, not only by characteristics and definition but also by results and fallout?

....
....
....
....
....

"He has not dealt with us as our sins deserve or repaid us according to our offenses" (v. 10). What factors complicate our ability to practice this kind of mercy toward others?

....
....
....
....
....

"The Lord has compassion on those who fear Him" (v. 13). God's "compassion" is not an emotional response but an act of deliberate strength. When are we called upon to do that?

....
....
....
....
....

Contemplating God in Salvation Over and Over Again

1. SALVATION HAS ALWAYS BEEN GOD'S PLAN FOR US.
2. SALVATION IS MADE POSSIBLE ONLY THROUGH CHRIST.
3. SALVATION MUST BE RECEIVED IN TOTAL DEPENDENCE.
4. SALVATION IS THE ULTIMATE ADOPTION PROCEDURE.
5. SALVATION GIVES US ACCESS TO THE HOLY SPIRIT.
6. SALVATION RESULTS IN THE FORGIVENESS OF OUR SINS.
   It's true that salvation is an objective fact, a defensible doctrine. But lest we ever think that defending it requires a briefcase full of books and charts and philosophical diagrams, remember that salvation is also an attractive benefit package. The lightness of a forgiven heart and the smile on a forgiven face can do a whole lot of your explaining for you.
7. SALVATION SAVES US FROM MORE THAN WE REALIZE.
8. SALVATION CONTINUES TO GROW AND TRANSFORM US.
9. SALVATION SHOULD BE A CONSTANT SOURCE OF JOY.
10. SALVATION IS BEST EXPERIENCED IN COMMUNITY.
11. SALVATION CROSSES ALL BORDERS AND BOUNDARIES.
12. SALVATION IS MEANT TO BE SHARED WITH OTHERS.
13. SALVATION IS AN EVERLASTING COVENANT WITH GOD.
14. SALVATION CULMINATES IN A FUTURE-TENSE EVENT.

Pray About

- What it means to fully, daily accept God's mercy and grace.
- How to let forgiven sins lead to a life marked by fewer sins.
- Those who are still living with the pain of guilt and shame.

SEVEN

BETTER THAN ADVERTISED

One of the most often heard yet least necessary confessions that you hear from many Christians is this: "I don't have much of a testimony to tell." No drugs. No gambling addiction. No 3:00 a.m. cry for help while waking up in a seedy, somewhere hotel and stumbling across Pat Robertson on television.

Yes, those stories pack great drama into the conversion experience and serve as an every-so-often reminder that no pit is too deep, no sin is too large—Jesus stops at nothing to arrest people's souls with his awesome salvation.

But if coming to Christ was more of a next logical step for you than a total one-eighty, if loving God was part of your makeup even before he made you over into his image, you don't have a thing to be ashamed of. In fact, you may possess something that many people would give nearly anything they own to enjoy, a gentleness and innocence that are impossible to acquire from the world and, even after redemption, can be hard to accept, hard to appropriate.

The myth of the storyless salvation is an outright lie because the measure of your worth in God's eyes is not what he's saved you *from* but what he's saved you *for*.

Lord God, I know a lot about what your salvation has done for me. But there's so much more I don't know and want to know.

If we have been joined with Him in the likeness of His death, we will certainly also be in the likeness of His resurrection. For we know that our old self was crucified with Him in order that sin's dominion over the body may be abolished, so that we may no longer be enslaved to sin, since *a person who has died is freed from sin's claims.* Now if we died with Christ, we believe that we will also live with Him, because we know that Christ, having been raised from the dead, no longer dies. Death no longer rules over Him. For in that He died, He died to sin once for all; but in that He lives, He lives to God. So, you too *consider yourselves dead to sin, but alive to God in Christ Jesus.*

Therefore do not let sin reign in your mortal body, so that you obey its desires. And do not offer any parts of it to sin as weapons for unrighteousness. But as those who are alive from the dead, *offer yourselves to God,* and all the parts of yourselves to God as weapons for righteousness. For sin shall not rule over you, because you are not under law but under grace.

Financial counselors often rate the soundness of a client's money decisions based not so much on profit and risk as on the *opportunity cost* of what those funds could potentially be doing. (Forgive me here—I'm already fast getting over my head.)

Let's say, for an easy example, that you have the option of spending $1,500 for a week's vacation with your family at the beach or putting that same $1,500 into an investment fund, dedicated to helping you pay for upcoming college expenses. The opportunity-cost calculation for how much your trip will actually set you back is not just the $1,500 you draw out of your savings but the amount that the $1,500 could grow to if left to mature.

Again you'd probably already figured this out.

Salvation, however, deserves to be viewed through this same lens. Being made right with God doesn't merely provide us with this, that, and the other thing. Our oneness with Christ has also protected us—and continues to protect us—from becoming the monster we could easily be without him.

It's a scenario we'd almost hate to imagine. Yet knowing it (if we could) would make us so much more thankful and aware and appreciative of what we've been given by God in salvation. I mean, think about the particular sins—the lusts, the coveting, the me-first demands—that never stop trying to deceive you. Try to picture who you might have been if you had nothing to hold you back but reputation and societal conventions. It's scary to think about.

> READ
> PHILIPPIANS 3:3–8

LIFE BEYOND MEASURE

For the majority of us who received Christ as kids and grew up within easy reach of his covenant promises, the "opportunity dividend" of following him over the course of sixty to eighty years can only be measured in miles and millions.

All the times since childhood when we've been able to read his Word, seek his counsel, and experience his Spirit. All the Sundays when we've shot down our excuses and found ourselves in church, letting worship remind us who we are and what's important. All the conversations we've had with our parents, our family, and dedicated believers who know him and love us and want nothing less than to lead us in truth.

How do you put a yardstick or a stopwatch on that? How do you quantify the value of one Christian lifetime? How do you assess the worth of the people you haven't harmed, the relationships you haven't devastated, the pain you haven't caused?

And yet just by virtue of the small amount of truth we actually put into practice as we imperfectly follow Christ, God's blessing gushes into every cell and molecule of our lives, soaking us in sweet satisfaction and splashing onto others as he brings them into our wake.

That's the beauty of the resurrection life, glimpses of glory that have seeped from heaven's gates and sloshed right into the middle of our own living rooms, painting our lives with colors many people never get to see or feel or react to.

READ
PSALM 16:5–11

SEEDS OF GREATNESS

How sad, then, that we so often miscalculate the magnitude of what God has done for us, declaring our lives boring when he has redeemed them from possibilities more scarred and scandalous than we'd ever expect ourselves capable of.

More than that, he has laid before us opportunities to continue growing in him, not merely being relieved at having avoided disaster but able to relish the new, daily developments his salvation initiates in our lives.

He has even gone before us, preparing us ahead of time for the trials that are still yet to come. Oh, although we dread the day when we perhaps—*perhaps*—will be forced to endure the death of a beloved spouse or the horror of wasting disease, we can celebrate already that because of our relationship with him, our battle will never be totally stripped of hope. His glorious salvation is even now redecorating our futures, not sparing us from all suffering but guaranteeing that each experience will be a fresh chance to love him, depend on him, and reflect his mighty power.

READ
PSALM 32:10–11

So never discount who you are as a child of God. Your testimony is as grand as anyone's.

DIG IN

Romans 6 reminds us that God hasn't just saved us from our **past** but has thrown wide the gates on our future.

"A PERSON WHO HAS DIED IS FREED FROM SIN'S CLAIMS" (v. 7). Yes, sin remains a nagging problem, but how do you **know** from experience that you are free from succumbing to it?

....
....
....
....
....

"CONSIDER YOURSELVES DEAD TO SIN, BUT ALIVE TO GOD IN CHRIST JESUS" (V. 11). This is much more than a mental exercise, but in what situations is this a deliberate choice of mind-sets?

....
....
....
....
....

"OFFER YOURSELVES TO GOD . . . AS WEAPONS FOR RIGHT-EOUSNESS" (V. 13). Think about the difference between **being** weapons against wickedness and "weapons for righteousness."

....
....
....
....
....

Contemplating God in Salvation Over and Over Again

1. Salvation has always been God's plan for us.

2. Salvation is made possible only through Christ.

3. Salvation must be received in total dependence.

4. Salvation is the ultimate adoption procedure.

5. Salvation gives us access to the Holy Spirit.

6. Salvation results in the forgiveness of our sins.

7. Salvation saves us from more than we realize.
   Our restoration in Christ is so much more dramatic and magnificent than we often realize. We should never cheapen or downplay what he has accomplished in us because it's the size of his gift that makes our salvation glorious. It's what keeps every one of us from ever being merely normal, for our lives have been declared extraordinary by the lover of our souls.

8. Salvation continues to grow and transform us.

9. Salvation should be a constant source of joy.

10. Salvation is best experienced in community.

11. Salvation crosses all borders and boundaries.

12. Salvation is meant to be shared with others.

13. Salvation is an everlasting covenant with God.

14. Salvation culminates in a future-tense event.

Pray About

- The perception of your own value and standing in Christ.
- Any feelings of inferiority that minimize your salvation.
- A new passion for becoming an active servant and follower.

EIGHT

MOVE-IN CONDITION

One of the hard choices to make when trying to sell your house is whether or not to put any more money into it than you already have—whether to leave cash allowances for potential buyers to paint their own rooms and lay their own carpet, or to go ahead and put in the sweat equity yourself.

But most realtors seem to agree—and most shoppers seem to want—a house they can just move into without a lot of remodeling and refurbishing.

Not so, the Holy Spirit.

The day we opened the door to his salvation, we invited him in to take measurements and handed him the credit card. We gave him full permission, not just to move things around but to gut the whole thing if he needed to—whatever it takes to make this place a suitable home for him to live in.

And until the day we die, he'll never stop working around the house—not because he's intent on cracking the whip but because he came here for a reason: to make our hearts a little more like Christ's every day.

Holy Spirit, I have received you into my heart knowing full well that it needs a lot of attention. Whatever you say, make me willing to do.

Rid yourselves of all wickedness, all deceit, hypocrisy, envy, and all slander. Like newborn infants, desire the unadulterated spiritual milk, *so that you may grow by it in your salvation,* since "you have tasted that the Lord is good."

Coming to Him, a living stone—rejected by men but chosen and valuable to God—*you yourselves,* as living stones, *are being built into a spiritual house* for a holy priesthood to offer spiritual sacrifices acceptable to God through Jesus Christ.

For it stands in Scripture: "Look! I lay a stone in Zion, a chosen and valuable cornerstone, and the one who believes in Him will never be put to shame!" So the honor is for you who believe; but for the unbelieving, "The stone that the builders rejected— this One has become the cornerstone," and "A stone that causes men to stumble, and a rock that trips them up." They stumble by disobeying the message; they were destined for this.

But you are "a chosen race, a royal priesthood, a holy nation, a people for His possession, *so that you may proclaim the praises" of the One who called you out of darkness* into His marvelous light. Once you were not a people, but now you are God's people; you had not received mercy, but now you have received mercy.

This has become a culture where it's pretty cool to be candid, to confess that we come up well short of the mark on most days, that the struggle of staying spiritual isn't a battle we win very often or even feel like fighting. Gone are the days when it was commonly expected that people might actually be who we thought they were. We're much more impressed now by active repentance than by actual, ongoing righteousness.

True, there's certainly a refreshing taste to all this.

But realizing that the daily practice of salvation is as hard for the next guy as it is for us—even the deacons, even the pastor—has the potential to make us quit trying very hard. Our fickle flesh being what it is, we can easily let such admissions keep us from shooting much higher than we have to. I mean, if our Sunday school teacher doesn't even do his devotions but once in a blue moon, who's to think we could do any better?

But wouldn't it be a lot more inspiring and contagious if, instead of walking around

READ
ROMANS 1:8–12

with this hangdog humility, we actually talked a little about the success God was growing in us? If we were really allowing Christ to go on a good winning streak in our lives, would we have a hard time saying much about it for fear we'd be setting ourselves a little too far apart from everyone else?

Is our ordinary-Joe exterior perhaps becoming just as much a façade as our spiritual pride used to be?

WORD UP

The apostle Paul was certainly not above mentioning the difficulties he had in following Christ. His Romans 7 treatise alone—"I do not practice what I want to do, but I do what I hate" (v. 15)—is enough to confirm that this honesty policy is a necessary part of our spiritual makeup. He was quick to confess that he dealt with "coveting of every kind" and a continual battle with the flesh (v. 8).

But as encouraging as this is to hear—especially for those of us who are a long way from Paul's brand of faith and fidelity—it doesn't mean we get to be content with failure. Paul could just as honestly tell you that he served God "with a clear conscience" (2 TIM. 1:3), that the believers of his day would do well to be "imitators" of him (1 COR. 4:16), that he sincerely wished everyone within the sound of his voice could "become as I am" (ACTS 26:29)—free in Christ and not afraid to admit it.

So when he told the church in Colossae to "put on heart-felt compassion, kindness, humility, gentleness, and patience" (COL. 3:12)—to continually allow Christ to clothe them in his genuine character traits of forgiveness, peace, and love—he wasn't just delivering a sermon. He wasn't treating these as impossible goals. He was telling them about something he was experiencing himself on a daily basis—not because *he* was anything special but because the Spirit inside him *really was!*

READ
PHILIPPIANS 2:12–16

PROOF OF PURCHASE

Just about all of those who are genuinely converted but who routinely find themselves questioning whether or not they're really saved, are usually dealing with the fact that these transforming qualities are not showing up in their daily lives. They're stuck wrangling with issues of basic faith when God has called them to start putting their multiplication tables to work.

In the Spirit's way of growing us, faith becomes goodness, becomes knowledge, becomes self-control, becomes endurance, becomes godliness, becomes brotherly affection, becomes love. "For if these qualities are yours and are increasing, they will keep you from being useless or unfruitful in the knowledge of our Lord Jesus Christ" (2 PET. 1:8).

But check this out: "The person who lacks these things is blind and shortsighted, and has forgotten the cleansing of his past sins" (V. 9). It's not that these offshoots of new growth have anything to do with saving you, but they do "confirm your calling and election" and keep you from being so susceptible to stumbling (V. 10).

READ
HEBREWS 6:9–12

Seeing real-live fruit on the tree is how Christians keep their hopes up.

DIG IN

Salvation is not a day but a lifetime, a lifestyle. And this chunk of I Peter 2 is a good way to remember that.

"SO THAT YOU MAY GROW BY IT IN YOUR SALVATION" (V. 2). Just as there are seasons of life, there are seasons of salvation. Where have you been seeing the growth happening lately?

....
....
....
....
....

"YOU YOURSELVES . . . ARE BEING BUILT INTO A SPIRITUAL HOUSE" (V. 5). Where does your "house" need the most work right now? The walls, the foundation, the roof, the windows?

....
....
....
....
....

"'SO THAT YOU MAY PROCLAIM THE PRAISES' OF THE ONE WHO CALLED YOU OUT OF DARKNESS" (V. 9). It's hard to be worshipful and resistant at the same time. Are you bucking at growing?

....
....
....
....
....

CONTEMPLATING GOD IN SALVATION OVER AND OVER AGAIN

1. SALVATION HAS ALWAYS BEEN GOD'S PLAN FOR US.
2. SALVATION IS MADE POSSIBLE ONLY THROUGH CHRIST.
3. SALVATION MUST BE RECEIVED IN TOTAL DEPENDENCE.
4. SALVATION IS THE ULTIMATE ADOPTION PROCEDURE.
5. SALVATION GIVES US ACCESS TO THE HOLY SPIRIT.
6. SALVATION RESULTS IN THE FORGIVENESS OF OUR SINS.
7. SALVATION SAVES US FROM MORE THAN WE REALIZE.
8. SALVATION CONTINUES TO GROW AND TRANSFORM US.
   The more imperceptible your lifestyles and attitudes are from those of the unsaved, the more your salvation is going to keep feeling fuzzy and synthetic. But as you let the Spirit start hammering and sawing on a daily basis, your life in Christ will take on a whole new meaning. For "whoever orders his conduct, I will show him the salvation of God" (Ps. 50:23).
9. SALVATION SHOULD BE A CONSTANT SOURCE OF JOY.
10. SALVATION IS BEST EXPERIENCED IN COMMUNITY.
11. SALVATION CROSSES ALL BORDERS AND BOUNDARIES.
12. SALVATION IS MEANT TO BE SHARED WITH OTHERS.
13. SALVATION IS AN EVERLASTING COVENANT WITH GOD.
14. SALVATION CULMINATES IN A FUTURE-TENSE EVENT.

PRAY ABOUT

- The genuineness of your character, mind-set, and testimony.
- The things that would help you submit to true transformation.
- What Christian love would look like on you and your family.

NINE

FEET OFF THE GROUND

Let's just say it like it is: being a Christian can be fun. That's not to say that it's *always* fun. It can be pretty tough in certain stretches. But so can everyone else's life, whether saved or otherwise. There are more than enough things working against us in this fallen world, not to mention the trouble we cause ourselves on a regular basis, to fully ensure that hardship and difficulty will come cycling around to all of us from time to time. Guaranteed.

But we Christians—heaven help us—we just get to enjoy life in ways that unbelievers have to miss out on.

For example, I've sat and watched the national Memorial Day concert on television and been proud to be an American. I've heard Tchaikovsky's Symphony No. 2 in person at the performing arts center downtown and been glad that my wife taught me there was more to music than Kenny Rogers.

But I've been in ordinary worship services where my heart got so warm, I thought it was going to catch my sport coat on fire. And it made Memorial Day and Tchaikovsky and Kenny Rogers all rolled together feel about as exciting as a clean pair of socks.

Lord Jesus, your love for me, your death for me, your new earth that's awaiting me . . . all I want to do is worship you.

PSALM 116:1-14

I love the LORD because He has heard my appeal for mercy. *Because He has turned His ear to me, I will call out to Him as long as I live.*

The ropes of death were wrapped around me, and the torments of Sheol overcame me; I encountered trouble and sorrow. Then I called on the name of the LORD: "LORD, save me!"

The LORD is gracious and righteous; our God is compassionate. The LORD guards the inexperienced; I was helpless, and He saved me. *Return to your rest, my soul, for the LORD has been good to you.* For you, LORD, rescued me from death, my eyes from tears, my feet from stumbling. I will walk before the LORD in the land of the living. I believed, even when I said, "I am severely afflicted." In my alarm I said, "Everyone is a liar."

How can I repay the LORD all the good He has done for me? I will take the cup of salvation and worship the LORD. I will fulfill my vows to the LORD in the presence of all His people.

I don't know how you feel most mornings when you wake up. Perhaps you suffer with chronic pain that catches in your back, neck, or feet before you've even raised yourself to the side of the bed. Perhaps you're under tremendous pressure at work, and the only thing worse than the insomnia of the night is the unwelcome light of day, knowing you're no more than a raisin bagel and a rush hour away from being back in the crosshairs all over again.

Perhaps the fresh air of morning feels fine for a few minutes before reality quickly begins to settle down around you like fifty-pound sandbags being thudded onto your shoulders: a rebellious son, a troubled marriage, a personal debt spiral, a medical test result.

Or perhaps you wake up most days feeling pretty spry and rested, looking forward to the duties and opportunities ahead, fairly aloof and unconcerned about anything serious, glad to know the coffee's made and the paper's in the driveway.

It really doesn't matter which of these scenes comes closest to describing your take on 6:00 a.m. Because whether you're emotionally weak, physically fatigued, happy as a lark, or not really thinking about it, salvation is your song to sing.

When you're loaded down with burdens, his redemption is the feather-light touch of forgiven sins. When you're unprepared to face the day, it's the reminder of resurrection power. And when you're just glad to see the sun and be alive, it's the good news that nothing really comes even close to knowing you're already alive forever.

> READ
> ISAIAH 60:18–20

HAPPY AND SAD

I confess, I haven't suffered nearly as much as some people have. By a long shot. But I've been through enough to know that as a believer in Christ, it is possible—it is our privilege, in fact—to be glad and to suffer at the same time.

I'm not saying that every day is necessarily a happy one. But I have woken up on mornings about as down as I can imagine. I've tried to pray and have only succeeded at getting myself more worried, more stressed, more ill at ease.

But I have opened my Bible and read again of God's glorious salvation, his path through the sea, his deliverance of his people. And I have seen the clouds break just enough for me to walk through. The circumstances didn't change. The problems still persisted. But my place in God's plan came through loud and clear again. And I've smiled when I felt like crying.

"For he will rescue the poor who cry out and the afflicted who have no helper. . . . He will redeem them from oppression and violence, for their lives are precious in his sight" (Ps. 72:12, 14). "The path of the righteous is level; You clear a straight path for the righteous. Yes, LORD, we wait for You in the path of Your judgments. Our desire is for Your name and renown" (ISA. 26:7–8).

READ
PSALM 95:1–7 A forgiven heart can handle anything. His saving love is our joy.

JOY AND STRENGTH

There are a lot of scary words in our common vocabulary:

· Cancer, heart failure, blood clots, strokes.
· Death, divorce, disease, dementia.
· Bankruptcy, foreclosure, creditors, liens.

There are also words that are less scary but still unsettling:

· Bad grades, teacher conferences, summer school.
· Conflict, deadlines, auditors, competition.
· Dishes, diapers, detergent, all-day duties.

But eternity colors everything. Salvation trumps it all. Though troubles have the power to wound and weaken, though trials have permission to scrape and claw, how can they destroy a person who has a zillion tomorrows in front of them? How many bad things can you do to a vapor, a dust speck, a person who's one-inch earthly and a million miles eternal?

So bring it on, life. We're under orders to overcome.

READ
1 JOHN 5:1–5

DIG IN

This great big God of ours has been in the delivery business for a long time and is still serving up joy right to our door see Psalm 116.

"BECAUSE HE HAS TURNED HIS EAR TO ME, I WILL CALL OUT TO HIM AS LONG AS I LIVE" (v. 2). Imagine how much harder the hard times would be if God wasn't willing to listen to us?

....
....
....
....
....

"RETURN TO YOUR REST, MY SOUL, FOR THE LORD HAS BEEN GOOD TO YOU" (v. 7). Gratitude is truly one of the great side benefits of salvation. How could you become a more thankful person?

....
....
....
....
....

"HOW CAN I REPAY THE LORD ALL THE GOOD HE HAS DONE FOR ME?" (v. 12). The literal answer, of course, is: "We can't." But what kind of actions on our part would indeed please him?

....
....
....
....
....

Contemplating God in Salvation Over and Over Again

1. Salvation has always been God's plan for us.
2. Salvation is made possible only through Christ.
3. Salvation must be received in total dependence.
4. Salvation is the ultimate adoption procedure.
5. Salvation gives us access to the Holy Spirit.
6. Salvation results in the forgiveness of our sins.
7. Salvation saves us from more than we realize.
8. Salvation continues to grow and transform us.
9. Salvation should be a constant source of joy.

    "We commend ourselves: . . . by the message of truth, by the power of God; through weapons of righteousness on the right hand and the left, . . . as unknown yet recognized; as dying and look—we live; as being chastened yet not killed; as grieving yet always rejoicing; as poor yet enriching many; as having nothing yet possessing everything" (2 Cor. 6:4, 7, 9–10).

10. Salvation is best experienced in community.
11. Salvation crosses all borders and boundaries.
12. Salvation is meant to be shared with others.
13. Salvation is an everlasting covenant with God.
14. Salvation culminates in a future-tense event.

Pray About

- Any joy leaks in your personal walk with Christ.
- Your own testimony as a follower of the one true God.
- What he's accomplishing through every single difficulty.

TEN

IN GROUPS
OF ONE

We could imagine life without church.

No budget committee meetings. No nursery duty. No turning off the Sunday morning news shows just when they're getting good. We could probably learn to like all of that.

But for all of its faults and inconveniences, the church continues to be a constant place of worship and learning, of companionship and accountability, of service and giving, of encouragement and respect.

Yes, there are certain seasons—and certain congregations—where each of these qualities becomes strained or nearly nonexistent. The teaching can become shoddy, the spirit can grow contentious, the caring can quit happening. But because the church is Christ's body and because he's established it as a source of community for his people and of light to the world, he keeps drawing it back into conformity with his design—if not from tip to tip, at least in various remnants and pockets.

So any believers who shortchange the church, or who consider it a take-or-leave cafeteria option, not only withhold themselves from the rest of us but also treat as unimportant a resource they'll never get too far in their Christian life without.

Lord God, I know how lonely and off base I can get when I'm out here on my own. Lead me to love your church all over again.

There is one body and one Spirit, just as you were called to one hope at your calling; one Lord, one faith, one baptism, one God and Father of all, who is above all and through all and in all.

Now grace was given to each one of us according to the measure of the Messiah's gift. . . .

He personally gave some to be apostles, some prophets, some evangelists, some pastors and teachers, *for the training of the saints in the work of ministry,* to build up the body of Christ, until we all reach unity in the faith and in the knowledge of God's Son, growing into a mature man with a stature measured by Christ's fullness. *Then we will no longer be little children,* tossed by the waves and blown around by every wind of teaching, by human cunning with cleverness in the techniques of deceit. But speaking the truth in love, *let us grow in every way into Him who is the head—Christ.* From Him the whole body, fitted and knit together by every supporting ligament, promotes the growth of the body for building up itself in love by the proper working of each individual part.

Just for the purposes of this little devotional, I'm going to assume that you and the church are friends. I know this isn't always the case for everyone, but maybe by looking again at what the Bible says about it, we can not only confirm and strengthen our own attachment to the body but also encourage those who are trying to subsist without it.

In this way we'd be doing one of the main things required of us in relating to the church: building it up, blessing its people.

If there was one thing the apostle Paul struggled with more than any other, I think it was the pain he had caused in persecuting believers. Whether or not this was his "thorn in the flesh" (2 COR. 12:7), I don't know. But you've got to figure Satan loved using this little number on Paul's mind, deep in the middle of a restless night, on each revisit to a city he had once passed through on blasphemer alert, every time he looked into the eyes of a widow whose husband he had picked off for martyrdom.

We do know for a fact that he considered himself "the least of the apostles, unworthy to be called an apostle, because I persecuted the church of God" (1 COR. 15:9).

That's because harming the church is a serious offense. And those who spend a good deal of their time finding fault with it are sure to miss the point of what church is all about.

READ
ROMANS 16:17–18

PULLED TIGHT

Look, if you get people involved in any undertaking, you're going to have some grit in the gears. It's the height of unreality to expect the church somehow to be perfect, to meet every need, to scratch every itch, to pull off everything in a way that pleases everybody.

Oh, how desperately your church needs today not someone who walks robotically in lockstep with every emphasis and decision but people like you who are there to be supportive, who truly care about one another, who know this thing is too important to be gunked up with their own tastes and preferences and side items.

When things start to get a little squirrelly or unimaginative in church, that's when a lot of believers just pull out, disengaging themselves from the experience, slowly cutting off their ties and cutting back on their investment. But actually we're needed most at times like these—needed to be an encouragement, needed to rally people's hearts, needed to keep our unifying salvation a front-page story and a top-drawer initiative.

We will never be 100 percent united around the building program or the summer youth plans or the Sunday schedule. But we are

READ
HEBREWS 10:23–25

exhorted and commanded to stay united in this: our oneness in Christ, our shared space at the foot of his cross.

59

Out of Many, One

That's because there's more going on at church than most of us usually realize. The splashy choir numbers are not just there to send shivers down our spine. The small prayer groups are not merely a place to empty our hearts and discuss things. The after-church get-togethers are not simply an excuse to eat too much and laugh with our friends.

Actually, you can get all that stuff somewhere else if you want to. Christians certainly don't hold the corner on good feelings or deep conversation.

But no other institution can be Christ's body—"the fullness of the One who fills all things in every way" (EPH. 1:23). No other organization is so vast and powerful that the supernatural, Spirit-led unity of its members makes even "the rulers and authorities in the heavens" marvel at what God can do (EPH. 3:10).

The church alone is the keeper of the mystery, the "pillar and foundation of the truth" (1 TIM. 3:15). The music and the messages and the meals and the missions committee are all serving the one purpose of embracing and expressing the saving love of God in Christ. They do it in different ways, like the brass and strings in a symphony. But when they all play their part, the music in God's ears is glorious.

By ourselves, none of us are any more than a reedy clarinet or a tinny piano, a magnet for catcalls and complaints. But together our lives become an ocean of worship, of service, of love within community.

READ
1 CORINTHIANS
12:21–27

Be there. Or be square.

DIG IN

Yes, there is great diversity between us. But as Ephesians 4 teaches, it makes our unity that much more impressive.

"FOR THE TRAINING OF THE SAINTS IN THE WORK OF MINISTRY" (V. 12). Salvation is a gift to be both cherished and shared. What "work of ministry" has Christ been calling you to?

....

....

....

....

....

"THEN WE WILL NO LONGER BE LITTLE CHILDREN" (V. 14). Just like having a running partner makes you stronger than you are alone, we grow best when we grow together. How?

....

....

....

....

....

"LET US GROW IN EVERY WAY INTO HIM WHO IS THE HEAD— CHRIST" (V. 15). What can you do to make sure that everything you're involved in at church really has this goal in mind?

....

....

....

....

....

Contemplating God in Salvation Over and Over Again

1. Salvation has always been God's plan for us.
2. Salvation is made possible only through Christ.
3. Salvation must be received in total dependence.
4. Salvation is the ultimate adoption procedure.
5. Salvation gives us access to the Holy Spirit.
6. Salvation results in the forgiveness of our sins.
7. Salvation saves us from more than we realize.
8. Salvation continues to grow and transform us.
9. Salvation should be a constant source of joy.
10. Salvation is best experienced in community.

    There are some who crave companionship and who consider this statement natural. But even those who prefer their own quiet can find that the community of faith has more than one way of operating. You don't have to be a tell-all to stay connected. You don't have to love parties to be a part. The fact that we all need one another doesn't mean we're all the same.

11. Salvation crosses all borders and boundaries.
12. Salvation is meant to be shared with others.
13. Salvation is an everlasting covenant with God.
14. Salvation culminates in a future-tense event.

Pray About

- Your own church—its needs, its focus, its leaders, its unity.
- Your own feelings toward and commitment to one another.
- The places where you pull away or perhaps push too hard.

ELEVEN

OUT OF THE ORDINARY

I t's the first night of vacation in a little resort town you've never been to before. You've checked in, you've wheeled your bags up to the room, you've stretched out on the bed for a second and taken in the view from the balcony. And now that everybody's freshened up and unfolded their legs from the trip, it's time to go out and see what's shaking in this place.

You don't know which streets connect to what, but that's OK. It's just fun to be here. You're making memories, enjoying the ride, not worried about getting back by any certain time.

And when you stop at the grocery after dinner to get some cereal and snacks and stuff, even though you're not used to the store and it takes twice as long to find half as much, so what? It's sort of an adventure.

Yes, as a rule, we don't prefer the unfamiliar. It takes work. It requires adjustments. It's costly and inconvenient. Sort of like when God tells us to take his salvation outside our personal space and territory. We don't really want to. Sounds dangerous.

Unless you look at unfamiliarity the right way.

Holy God, I don't just naturally gravitate toward the unexpected and the out of the way. Has comfort become an unspoken way of life for me?

"In truth, I understand that God doesn't show favoritism, but *in every nation the person who fears Him* and does righteousness *is acceptable to Him.* He sent the message to the sons of Israel, proclaiming the good news of peace through Jesus Christ—He is Lord of all. You know the events that took place throughout all Judea, beginning from Galilee after the baptism that John preached: how God appointed Jesus of Nazareth with the Holy Spirit and with power, and how he went about doing good and curing all who were under the tyranny of the Devil, because God was with Him. We ourselves are witnesses of everything He did in both the Judean country and in Jerusalem; yet they killed Him by hanging Him on a tree. *God raised up this man on the third day and permitted Him to be seen,* not by all the people, but by us, witnesses appointed beforehand by God, who ate and drank with Him after He rose from the dead. He commanded us to preach to the people, and to solemnly testify that He is the One appointed by God to be the Judge of the living and the dead. All the prophets testify about Him that through His name *everyone who believes in Him will receive forgiveness of sins.*"

What do these things have in common? A maximum security prison in the hills of east Tennessee. The dirt floor under a grass hut in a tribal African village. The snarled traffic and bustling business district of downtown Tokyo. The family farm on six hundred sprawling acres in western Iowa. The temporary tent cities at an annual horse race in Mongolia. A quaint little townhouse in Seattle.

Answer: they're all "the ends of the earth" for somebody.

And you know what? So was *our* century and street address when the psalmist wrote that "all the ends of the earth have seen our God's victory" (Ps. 98:3)—or when Isaiah prophesied, "All the ends of the earth will see the salvation of our God" (Isa. 52:10).

We were out there. *Way* out there. The great unknown. The far-distant lands. The weirdos who plunk down three dollars or more just to sit around Starbucks, who spritz deodorant under our arms, who eat with silver instead of our fingers.

And yet in God's good mercy and perfect timing, the flood-waters of Christian faith found their way to our shores, to our hemisphere, to our hometown forefathers and the country lanes of our culture. Salvation gleamed its light with a brightness we could see from even as far afield as our own historical outpost. And we foreigners became naturalized through the welcoming blood of Jesus Christ.

READ
EPHESIANS 2:12–13

ALL FOR ONE

Much of the New Testament, of course, is taken up with this big-tent mentality, that God through Christ has "proclaimed the good news of peace to you who were far away and peace to those who were near" (EPH. 2:17), that Jesus is "the true light, who gives light to everyone" (JOHN 1:9).

This was news to the people of Jesus' day. Or at least it was to those who hadn't been listening very well. The historical record told of some Ruths and Rahabs along the way—outsiders who had been received into the fold of the faithful. Even as far back as the early days of Israelite lore, Jacob had prophesied, "The scepter will not depart from Judah, or the staff from between his feet, until He whose right it is comes and *the obedience of the peoples* belongs to Him" (GEN. 49:10)—a foresighted reference to Christ.

Oh, there were some who were paying attention. Simeon, who cradled the baby Jesus in his arms and said in praise to God, "My eyes have seen Your salvation. You have prepared it in the presence of all peoples—a light for revelation to the Gentiles and glory to Your people Israel" (LUKE 2:30–32).

But all too often in the pages of Scripture, we see only the bigotry and hypocrisy in the fat faces of the Pharisees, those who simply could not tolerate the notion that half-breeds and heretics could ever fit into the robes of the righteous.

Yet in the words and squinty glances of the legalists, we see too much of ourselves. And I hope it scares us. It should.

READ
ACTS 28:25–29

OH YEAH?

I mean, poking fun at the Pharisees is easy. We're people of acceptance now. We've lived through the civil rights movement. Everyone's equal, man. You can read about it in our editorial pages.

Yes, that's probably true. We're by and large much more accepting of other races and religions than we were in days past. But is that the only prejudice known to man?

Would I believe it if some well-known Hollywood actor came to Christ? Would I not first consider it a publicity stunt or an attempt to prop up a fading career?

Do I really think the old high school friend who owns his own company and just bought a half-million dollar house in a posh, gated community would consider himself in great need of a Savior?

I may believe in my mind that Jesus came for the homeless, the slob, the rude, the embarrassing, the nursing home resident, the sagging skateboarder. But do I believe it enough to mention it when the Spirit puts me up close with these people? Usually not.

So is my enlightened, twenty-first-century spirituality a whole lot different from the Pharisees of old? Or am I truly a living

READ
LUKE 3:3–6

testimony to the belief that God's salvation is much wider and broader than I used to think it was?

DIG IN

Even the apostle Peter wasn't all that quick to open his arms to the Gentiles, until God drew him a picture in Acts 10.

"IN EVERY NATION THE PERSON WHO FEARS HIM . . . IS ACCEPTABLE TO HIM" (v. 35). If this is true—that God is accepting of the unacceptable—what keeps us from being so inviting?

....

....

....

....

....

"GOD RAISED UP THIS MAN ON THE THIRD DAY AND PERMITTED HIM TO BE SEEN" (v. 40). In what ways do you keep your salvation under wraps? What are the motivations behind that?

....

....

....

....

....

"EVERYONE WHO BELIEVES IN HIM WILL RECEIVE FORGIVENESS OF SINS" (v. 43). What did God mean by saying "everyone"? And what do we mean by not always believing it?

....

....

....

....

....

Contemplating God in Salvation Over and Over Again

1. Salvation has always been God's plan for us.
2. Salvation is made possible only through Christ.
3. Salvation must be received in total dependence.
4. Salvation is the ultimate adoption procedure.
5. Salvation gives us access to the Holy Spirit.
6. Salvation results in the forgiveness of our sins.
7. Salvation saves us from more than we realize.
8. Salvation continues to grow and transform us.
9. Salvation should be a constant source of joy.
10. Salvation is best experienced in community.
11. Salvation crosses all borders and boundaries.
    We are the wall builders. We are the dividing liners. We are the keeper-outers who often don't speak unless spoken to and don't go if we don't feel like it. But Jesus is the barrier destroyor. He is the curtain puller-downer. He is the international collector who brings them in from Germany and Jamaica, from Canada and Croatia, from Albuquerque and Albania. From everywhere.
12. Salvation is meant to be shared with others.
13. Salvation is an everlasting covenant with God.
14. Salvation culminates in a future-tense event.

Pray About

- What would need to change in you to live this doctrine.
- Who the "everyones" are who live within your world.
- Where God may be calling you to go to declare him.

TWELVE

LET'S HEAR IT

Mark has been a recent convert to the new health and fitness craze. He's dropped about fifteen pounds and an inch or two around his middle, just by walking a couple of miles a day and cutting back on late-night snacks and potato chips. And he's absolutely sure his plan would work for me.

Kelly's getting married later this summer. Her boyfriend popped the question over a Valentine's Day dinner, and she's hardly come down off the ceiling since. They'll be staying in town while she finishes school this fall, but they hope to relocate once she's done. She's sure it'll all work out somehow. It's a pretty exciting time for her.

Ben and Stephen are thinking about starting their own graphic design company. They've been dreaming about it for two years now, and they believe they've finally come up with enough clout and clients to make it a go. Some of their friends think they're nuts for doing it. But you never know till you try. They're really serious about giving it a shot.

Know how I know all these things? Because they matter to these people. And because they told me.

Lord Jesus, your salvation means everything to me. But I need help remembering that others need you too. Let them see you in me.

"God has resurrected this Jesus. We are all witnesses of this. Therefore, since He has been exalted to the right hand of God and has received from the Father the promised Holy Spirit, He has poured out what you both see and hear. For it was not David who ascended into the heavens, but he himself says, 'The Lord said to my Lord, "Sit at My right hand until I make Your enemies Your footstool."'

"Therefore let all the house of Israel know with certainty that God has made this Jesus, whom you crucified, both Lord and Messiah."

When they heard this, they were *pierced to the heart* and said to Peter and the rest of the apostles: "Brothers, what must we do?"

"Repent," Peter said to them, "and be baptized, each of you, in the name of Jesus the Messiah for the forgiveness of your sins, and you will receive the gift of the Holy Spirit. For the promise is for you and for your children, and for all who are far off, as many as the Lord our God will call." And *with many other words he testified and strongly urged them,* saying, "Be saved from this corrupt generation!"

Telling others about Christ is scary primarily because it can make for uncomfortable conversation and because we might be asked something we don't know. We'd much rather be thought nice and be approved of than run the risk of offending someone or looking stupid.

So we don't. Very often.

And as a result, the salvation we love so much, the forgiveness of sins we're so relieved about, the hope of heaven we're so assured of, stays bottled up inside us with nowhere to go. Yes, worship allows us to vent its joy somewhat. But because we were created to need companionship and camaraderie, something vital turns up missing when this crucial, consuming aspect of our lives is hushed up and off limits.

It's like holding your breath or trying to staunch a sneeze. There's a constipation factor at work in all of this.

So in an effort to avoid the discomfort of what feels like confrontation, we wind up with the blahs of guilt and shame and hypocrisy. It's terrible.

And because we're afraid of being outsmarted or made to feel narrow, we choke down what we do know and only succeed in becoming *more* narrow, not letting our knowledge breathe the air of real life.

READ
LUKE 9:57–62

FIRST LOVE

But just as there seem to be two great fears that stifle our sharing, there are two great truths and encouragements that can motivate us to obedience.

Jesus, of course, put them better than anyone. "Which commandment is the most important of all?" someone asked him one day. "Love the Lord your God," he answered, and "love your neighbor as yourself. There is no other commandment greater than these" (MARK 12:28, 30–31).

So the first and most natural way to keep Christ in our conversation is to make sure he's our food and drink, our meat and bread, our Lord in private and our Friend at all times. To love him.

In the passage you just read from Luke 9, Jesus rebuked the one who asked to "go bury my father" (v. 59). Most likely this dodge didn't mean that his dad was actually dead and awaiting interment. This guy just wasn't really ready yet to give up the "dead" pursuits of his everyday lifestyle. Yeah, Jesus might have been an adventurous tag-on for him, a cool conversation piece. But he wasn't this man's true desire.

And until he is for us, we'll always find ourselves talking a lot more about movies and football and the high price of gasoline than about the one thing that matters most to us.

READ
PSALM 71:14–19

CARING ENOUGH

The second secret, as Jesus said, is our love for others. I mean, how many times, in all the listings and teachings and exhortations of the Bible does the writer of a particular book or letter sum up his inspired wording by saying, *"The main thing is to love."*

Honestly, we worry too much about what we should say to people, how we should respond to a particular objection, what we should lead off with and worry about. Sharing the truth and life of Christ's salvation is actually more about listening than it is about talking. Listening to what people are saying. Listening for the needs of their hearts. Listening as they mention what's important to them.

And listening as the Spirit puts this whole thing together.

He will, you know. He hasn't been having you reading in Romans this week just because it's what *you* needed to hear. He didn't give you a spiritual insight as you were weeding your flowerbed just because he thought you'd like it. He wasn't drawing your attention to a particular news item just because you were bored and didn't have anything else to do.

The Holy Spirit prepares us for these encounters with others. He stands with us and strengthens us (2 TIM. 4:17). "For God

READ
COLOSSIANS
4:2–6

has not given us a spirit of fearfulness, but one of power, love, and sound judgment" (2 TIM. 1:7).

And to him be all the glory.

DIG IN

It hadn't been six weeks since Peter was denying he even knew Jesus. God can use any of us to proclaim his salvation. See Acts 2.

"GOD HAS RESURRECTED THIS JESUS. WE ARE ALL WITNESSES OF THIS" (V. 32). What have you seen in just the last week or two that's reminded you again how precious your Savior is?

....
....
....
....
....

"WHEN THEY HEARD THIS, THEY WERE PIERCED TO THE HEART" (V. 37). If we knew this would happen as a result of our witness, we'd do it more often. Why don't we believe it will?

....
....
....
....
....

"WITH MANY OTHER WORDS HE TESTIFIED AND STRONGLY URGED THEM" (V. 40). How do you marry the biblical concepts of "strongly" urging and being "gracious" in conversation?

....
....
....
....
....

Contemplating God in Salvation Over and Over Again

1. Salvation has always been God's plan for us.
2. Salvation is made possible only through Christ.
3. Salvation must be received in total dependence.
4. Salvation is the ultimate adoption procedure.
5. Salvation gives us access to the Holy Spirit.
6. Salvation results in the forgiveness of our sins.
7. Salvation saves us from more than we realize.
8. Salvation continues to grow and transform us.
9. Salvation should be a constant source of joy.
10. Salvation is best experienced in community.
11. Salvation crosses all borders and boundaries.
12. Salvation is meant to be shared with others.

    Paul said evangelism was the "aim" of his life (Rom. 15:20), that he and his compadres were "ambassadors for Christ" (2 Cor. 5:20). Some say this was his special calling, just as it is for a select handful today. But you wait till the Spirit draws someone to Christ right in front of your eyes. And see if you want to keep delegating this joy to somebody else.

13. Salvation is an everlasting covenant with God.
14. Salvation culminates in a future-tense event.

Pray About

- Continually having an everyday experience of God's grace.
- Receiving the courage to bring Christ into conversation.
- What love for others, especially the unsaved, really means.

THIRTEEN

ROCK SOLID

I could add up on both hands and both feet (with the addition of your hands and your feet) the number of times I've started something and haven't finished it.

The great attic purge and reorganization of 1997. The church prayer ministry initiative I drew up on paper and mapped out by priority, schedule, and category. The nine-volume *History of Civilization* my Uncle Joe bought for me and sent down from Minnesota.

I could go on. Easily. Without notes. Total stream of consciousness. The computer cataloging of our medical histories and financial accounts. The lists of *Andy Griffith* episodes and TV movies on our mountain of unmarked VHS tapes. The two books whose first two chapters are both stored on my hard drive.

But God, on the other hand, has never started anything he didn't finish. That includes making a new daddy out of a hundred-year-old geezer named Abraham, a conquering nation out of a crop of Egyptian slaves, and a king out of a shepherd boy. Not to mention sending his own Son down into the grave and back again.

Oh, and saving someone like us.

Lord God, may I never doubt that your salvation is mine for keeps, not because I'm worthy to receive it but because you're faithful to ensure it.

ISAIAH 51:1, 4–9

Listen to Me, you who pursue righteousness, you who seek the LORD: *Look to the rock from which you were cut,* and to the quarry from which you were dug. . . .

Pay attention to Me, My people, and listen to Me, My nation; for instruction will come from Me, and My justice for a light to the nations. I will bring it about quickly. My righteousness is near; My salvation appears, and My arms will bring justice to the nations. The coastlands will put their hope in Me, and they will look to My strength. Look up to the heavens, and look at the earth beneath; for the heavens will vanish like smoke, the earth will wear out like a garment, and its inhabitants will die in like manner. *But My salvation will last forever,* and My righteousness will never be shattered.

Listen to Me, you who know righteousness, the people in whose heart is My instruction: do not fear disgrace by men, and do not be shattered by their taunts. For the moth will devour them like a garment, and the worm will eat them like wool. But My righteousness will last forever, and My salvation for all generations.

Wake up, wake up! Put on the strength of the LORD's power.

There's probably not a Christian alive who at one time or another hasn't wondered to himself whether or not this thing is really true. Even though we don't live on blind faith (what with the many proofs and evidences of the Bible's authenticity), we still have lots of questions we don't know the answers to. And so on the occasional off Friday, in an occasional odd numbered year, when things aren't stacking up very well . . . the thought can cross your mind.

No, that doesn't make the thought true. But it's not impossible to think it.

There are many people also, while in this questioning mood, who can allow themselves to become convinced they're not really saved.

And it makes me feel tired just about every time I hear that question because it seems to me that nearly everyone who would care about the answer—a person who's wanting to be assured of God's approval—is indicating merely by asking it that his heart is turned toward the Lord.

God doesn't draw people to himself just to check them out and examine their test scores. The Bible is so clear that we are saved through Christ's righteousness alone, that none of our do-goods factor into the equation. So if he has reached out to us in his mercy and compassion, and we have responded to him in honest faith, this question of "are we in or are we out" can be settled in our hearts forever. Really.

READ
HEBREWS 8:10–12

SUPER GLUE

It appears that David perhaps had the best perspective on all this. His insightful Psalm 69 indicates that he knew he was rightly accused of "foolishness" and "guilty acts"—negligent and deliberate sins that were "not hidden" from God's sight (v. 5).

He knew also what it was like to come under the heavy hand of others' opinions, to be insulted and disgraced and made to feel like an imposter in the house of God.

He knew as well how it felt to be "sunk in deep mud" (v. 2), to be so worn out from battle and hardship and the role of the hunted that his eyes could fail, "looking for my God" (v. 3), nearly assured that he'd really been abandoned this time.

Part of his brain told him that he likely deserved these desperate emotions, that he was probably right in thinking that his faith had been an invisible, cleverly disguised lie. Another part of him seemed to say that it was totally up to *him* to get his good feelings back, that maybe if he tossed God a bone—"an ox," maybe, "a bull with horns and hooves" (v. 31)—this religious deed might put him back on God's good side.

"But as for me—poor and in pain—let your salvation protect me, God. I will praise God's name with song and exalt Him with thanksgiving . . . for the LORD listens to the needy and does not despise His own" (vv. 29, 33).

He loves you so much, dear child of heaven. Believe him—you're not going anywhere.

READ
2 TIMOTHY 2:11–13

HERE TO STAY

Sometimes, of course, this question of whether or not someone's salvation has actually taken isn't asked in reference to the asker but about someone else he loves and cares for, a person who at one time gave evidence of Christian faith but who hasn't appeared (from the best we can tell) to have much to do with God since.

And, yes, that is troubling. A tree should be known by its fruit, the Scripture says. Genuine faith should result in a genuine difference, an identifiable lifestyle.

Yes, there are those who, having turned their back on us, have indicated that "they did not belong to us; for if they had belonged to us, they would have remained with us" (1 JOHN 2:19). But in the end we are clearly warned by God not to judge anyone's eternal status with him. We can keep praying, we can keep loving, we can keep asking them over for dinner and daring to voice our concern.

But God's covenant with his kids is an eternal, unbreakable one. And though we all go through seasons and Saturdays where we don't look the least bit saved, Jesus knows the ones who are his.

READ
1 JOHN 5:12–13

And "no one will snatch them out of My hand" (JOHN 10:28).

DIG IN

Isaiah had this stuck-like-glue salvation teaching down long before we got to worrying about it. His chapter 51 spells it out.

"LOOK TO THE ROCK FROM WHICH YOU WERE CUT" (V. 1). What's a cut stone compared to a quarry? Or a drop to an ocean? And what makes us think our salvation is all up to us?

....

....

....

....

....

"BUT MY SALVATION WILL LAST FOREVER" (V. 6). It's not really our salvation. It's his. It's not our righteousness. It's his. Does this have any impact on the living-out of the Christ life?

....

....

....

....

....

"WAKE UP, WAKE UP! PUT ON THE STRENGTH OF THE LORD'S POWER" (V. 9). Wouldn't that be a good way to start things every morning? How could you appropriate his saving strength?

....

....

....

....

....

Contemplating God in Salvation Over and Over Again

1. Salvation has always been God's plan for us.
2. Salvation is made possible only through Christ.
3. Salvation must be received in total dependence.
4. Salvation is the ultimate adoption procedure.
5. Salvation gives us access to the Holy Spirit.
6. Salvation results in the forgiveness of our sins.
7. Salvation saves us from more than we realize.
8. Salvation continues to grow and transform us.
9. Salvation should be a constant source of joy.
10. Salvation is best experienced in community.
11. Salvation crosses all borders and boundaries.
12. Salvation is meant to be shared with others.
13. Salvation is an everlasting covenant with God.

    Probably the best way to close this out is to hear from someone who really understood it. "Is it not true my house is with God? For He has established an everlasting covenant with me, ordered and secured in every detail. Will He not bring about my whole salvation and my every desire?" (2 Sam. 23:5). And can he not be trusted to do the same with us?

14. Salvation culminates in a future-tense event.

Pray About

- Trusting God's Word when it says we're safe with him.
- Keeping his mercy and grace before you every single day.
- How to encourage those who have such trouble trusting.

FOURTEEN
WAIT AND SEE

We don't know the half of it.

God's salvation has been so good to us up to this point. We've grown with it. We've been changed by it. It's kept us going on days when we didn't think we had anything left to give.

But I'm telling you, our salvation is just warming up.

Ask a high school athlete how spring practice compares to a Friday night playoff game in November. Ask a family who's gone on vacation in Colorado how renting and hauling and putting on the gear compares to finally getting out there on the slopes and skiing. Ask yourself how Christmas shopping compares to Christmas morning.

Whatever beauty and blessing we enjoy from salvation on an average Sunday is like the first bite of a candy bar, like the first day of fall, like the first glint of sunrise, like the first ride home with your new puppy.

God's goodness is all around us. On most days we can even feel it.

But get ready. His best is yet to come.

Lord God, there are times when I feel more secure in you than others. But help me always to know by faith that you've already taken care of everything.

According to the law almost everything is purified with blood, and *without the shedding of blood there is no forgiveness.*

Therefore it was necessary for the copies of the things in the heavens to be purified with these sacrifices, but the heavenly things themselves to be purified with better sacrifices than these. For the Messiah did not enter a sanctuary made with hands (only a model of the true one) but into heaven itself, *that He might now appear in the presence of God for us.* He did not do this to offer Himself many times, as the high priest enters the sanctuary yearly with the blood of another. Otherwise, He would have had to suffer many times since the foundation of the world. But now He has appeared one time, at the end of the ages, for the removal of sin by the sacrifice of Himself.

And just as it is appointed for people to die once—and after this, judgment—so also the Messiah, having been offered once to bear the sins of many, will appear a second time, not to bear sin, but *to bring salvation to those who are waiting for Him.*

The longer we're here, the more proclivity we have for living in the past. As we begin to age and the firing of short-term memory becomes less fluid and reliable, scenes from the distant past can start to seem almost more real to us than the ham sandwich we're having for lunch. It can become easier to recall a scene from our childhood than to remember where we left our glasses.

(I wish I didn't speak from such experience.)

But one of the great distinctives of Christianity is that it comes with a capacity for living in the future—not based on wishful thinking, not tied to holistic hopes, but anchored in truth, promised by a God who hasn't broken one yet.

Yes, we know our salvation occurred in the past. God's eternal plan decreed it, his Son secured it, we remember the day we received it.

We also know that his salvation is happening in us right now. We've seen him clean sins from our lives that we never thought we could live without. We've experienced him rescuing us from huge messes we'd caused and restoring us to his perfect will. We've sensed the change in us—from who we were to who we are.

And with that same assurance and confidence, we can already know today that our salvation is coming in the future, on that great and glorious day when the one we've believed becomes the one we behold— right in front of our faces, fresh within view, everything we've dreamed . . . and so much more.

READ
ROMANS 13:11–14

GLORY, GLORY

This is the biblical doctrine of *glorification*—the final reward and reality of our salvation. "Those He predestined, He also called; and those He called, He also justified; and those He justified, He also glorified" (ROM. 8:30).

And the last is just as certain as the first.

We don't know exactly what being glorified will be like. Many people speculate, drawing insights from the Scriptures to piece together our experience in paradise. It's fun to imagine—no sin, no sadness, no dread, no death. The prospect of reconnecting with old friends and family members. The freedom from feeling even the slightest hint of disease or deterioration. Never again having to hide our kids' eyes at the video store or worry about how they're doing or where they're going. Never needing to plan for retirement or write new clauses into our wills based on who might predecease whom.

Imagine taking all concept of time out of our living arrangement. We could be ready to start right now!

But even with all we don't know, we do know that our true "citizenship is in heaven, from which we also eagerly wait for a Savior, the Lord Jesus Christ. He will transform the body of our humble condition into the likeness of His glorious body, by the power that enables Him to subject everything to Himself"

READ
COLOSSIANS 3:1–4

(PHIL. 3:20–21).

And we will be saved. Forever and ever secure.

FAITHFUL TO THE END

All of this is based on one thing: the absolute faithfulness of God.

And if we're not willing to rest in that, then we'd better be able to name at least one thing that's more worthy of our confidence. Our very life would depend on it.

I know heaven can feel so distant and uncertain at times. The whole story of the Bible is the long wait for his rescue and deliverance: "My eyes grow weary looking for Your salvation and for Your righteous promise" (Ps. 119:123). "I wait for the LORD; I wait, and put my hope in His word" (Ps. 130:5).

But there is something—and Someone—at the end of our waiting. Promise. "I am sure of this, that He who started a good work in you will carry it on to completion until the day of Christ Jesus" (PHIL. 1:6). "He will also confirm you to the end, blameless in the day of our Lord Jesus Christ. God is faithful" (1 COR. 1:8–9).

And so the salvation that started before time began, and is still ticking along with your wristwatch at this very moment, is awaiting the perfect day to finally show itself.

Never doubt it. Be ready. Keep looking. He's coming.

READ
1 THESSALONIANS
5:23–24

DIG IN

Hebrews 9 runs the rapids from Moses to the Messiah and right past our modern times to a sure and coming day

"WITHOUT THE SHEDDING OF BLOOD THERE IS NO FORGIVENESS" (v. 22). This has always been the way in God's order of things. How can our trust in his past assist our trust in his future?

....

....

....

....

"THAT HE MIGHT NOW APPEAR IN THE PRESENCE OF GOD FOR US" (v. 24). Two of the greatest words in Scripture are the words "for us." Think of what they mean from such a big God.

....

....

....

....

....

"TO BRING SALVATION TO THOSE WHO ARE WAITING FOR HIM" (v. 28). What should our waiting look like and be seen as? And how can we encourage one another to do it better?

....

....

....

....

....

Experiencing God in Salvation Over and Over Again

1. Salvation has always been God's plan for us.
2. Salvation is made possible only through Christ.
3. Salvation must be received in total dependence.
4. Salvation is the ultimate adoption procedure.
5. Salvation gives us access to the Holy Spirit.
6. Salvation results in the forgiveness of our sins.
7. Salvation saves us from more than we realize.
8. Salvation continues to grow and transform us.
9. Salvation should be a constant source of joy.
10. Salvation is best experienced in community.
11. Salvation crosses all borders and boundaries.
12. Salvation is meant to be shared with others.
13. Salvation is an everlasting convenant with God.
14. Salvation culminates in a future-tense event.
    Heaven is real. And the hope of our final redemption is more sure than the afternoon mail or the warmth of our favorite sweatshirt. "On that day it will be said, 'Look, this is our God; we have waited for Him, and He has saved us. . . . Let us rejoice and be glad in His salvation'" (Isa. 25:9). If we really believe that, why not start the rejoicing right now?

Pray About

- Anything that keeps you from walking in Christ's assurance.
- People you know who are drying up inside from lack of hope.
- Staying ready, faithful, and watching for the Lord's appearing.

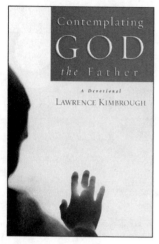

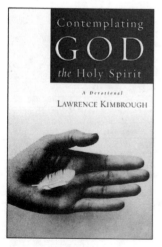
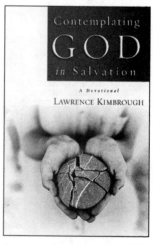